INSIDE THE NFL
AFC SOUTH

THE HOUSTON TEXANS

THE INDIANAPOLIS COLTS

THE JACKSONVILLE JAGUARS

THE TENNESSEE TITANS

BY BRIAN PETERSON

The Child's World®

Published in the United States of America by
The Child's World® • 1980 Lookout Drive
Mankato, MN 56003-1705
800-599-READ • www.childsworld.com

ACKNOWLEDGEMENTS
The Child's World®: Mary Berendes,
Publishing Director

The Design Lab: Kathleen Petelinsek,
Design; Gregory Lindholm, Page Production

Manuscript consulting and photo research
by Shoreline Publishing Group LLC.

PHOTOS
Cover: Joe Robbins (front and back)
Interior: AP/Wide World: 5, 6, 9, 12, 20, 23, 25,
26, 27, 31; Corbis: 16; Joe Robbins: 13, 15, 19,
28, 32.

LIBRARY OF CONGRESS
CATALOGING-IN-PUBLICATION DATA

Peterson, Brian C.
    AFC South / by Brian Peterson.
        p. cm. — (Inside the NFL)
    Includes bibliographical references and index.
    ISBN 978-1-60253-003-4
(library bound : alk. paper)
    1. National Football League—History—Juvenile
literature. 2. Football—United States—History—
Juvenile literature. I. Title. II. Series.
    GV955.5.N35P48 2008
    796.332'640973—dc22   2008010521

TABLE OF CONTENTS

TABLE OF CONTENTS

AFC SOUTH
INTRODUCTION

T he four teams in the AFC South follow an old saying heard at weddings. Brides, goes the saying, are supposed to wear "something old, something new, something borrowed, and something blue."

There are two "old" teams in this division and two very new ones. There are two teams that have been permanently "borrowed" from other cities by their current cities. And there are three teams that feature blue in their uniforms.

The Colts and Titans are old, but they've made some big moves. The Colts first played in Baltimore in 1953, but moved to Indianapolis in 1984. They are the only AFC South team to win a **Super Bowl** (one in Baltimore and one in Indianapolis). The Tennessee Titans used to be the Houston Oilers, who started in 1960. And the new team? That's the Houston Texans, who started play in 2002.

Only one AFC South team, the Jacksonville Jaguars, has remained in its original home city. Attention trivia fans: The Jaguars are also the only team in the division that doesn't have blue in its uniforms.

Read on to find out more about this unique quartet of NFL teams.

The AFC South is a very good division. Three of its four clubs made the **playoffs** in the 2007 season.

CHAPTER ONE
THE HOUSTON TEXANS

The state of Texas is known for its love affair with football. Because of that, it wasn't a big surprise when the city of Houston was awarded an NFL **expansion team** to begin play in 2002. Houston beat out Los Angeles to serve as home for the league's 32nd **franchise.**

Both cities were used to having NFL teams. Los Angeles had been home to the Rams from 1946 to 1994, when they moved to St. Louis. The Raiders played in L.A., too, from 1982 to 1994, before moving back to Oakland. Houston hosted the Oilers from 1960 to 1996, but they moved to Tennessee (see page 27). Both cities had NFL history on their side, and both had ownership groups with lots of money. In the end, though, Houston promised to build a stadium, and that made the difference.

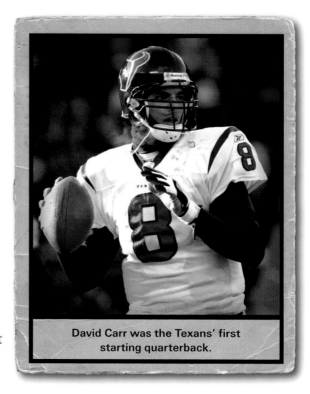

David Carr was the Texans' first starting quarterback.

When Houston was announced in 1999 as the winner of the new team, the city erupted with cheers. It had missed pro football since the Oilers left. Now, new owner Bob McNair was ready to make Houston a pro football hotbed again. He had to spend a record $700 million for the privilege of doing this. And the city of Houston had to help him build a brand-new stadium for his new team.

McNair and his **associates** got right to work. Their first employee was a longtime NFL general manager named Charley Casserly. Casserly had been a key executive with the Washington Redskins when that team won several Super Bowls. Casserly spent the next year preparing every part of the team, from the uniforms to the training facilities. Finally, in January 2001, he hired former Carolina Panthers head coach Dom Capers to be the team's first head coach. By the end of 2001, the team had signed its first **free agents** and was preparing for its first NFL **draft** in April 2002.

Capers emphasized defense, knowing that that skill can often be easier to master more quickly. If he could keep other teams from scoring too much, he might have just enough offense to win a few games. After several preseason games, the team finally was ready to play its first regular-season game on September 8, 2002.

Reliant Stadium was filled with more than 69,000 fans, all eager to see the Texans play their in-state **rival**, the Dallas Cowboys. Quarterback David Carr from Fresno State, who had been the team's first-ever college draft choice and the first overall selection in the 2002 NFL draft, came out smoking. He threw a 19-yard touchdown pass to tight end Billy Miller for the team's first touchdown. Capers' plan of playing tough defense paid off. Dallas quarterback Quincy Carter rarely had time to operate.

Incredibly, the Texans defeated the Cowboys 19–10 to become the first NFL expansion team to win its first game since the Minnesota Vikings did it in 1961.

Although the team finished with only four wins in that first season, two of its players earned coveted spots in the Pro Bowl, the NFL's yearly all-star game. The Texans improved in 2003 with five wins. But the big news was running back Domanick Davis, who gained 1,031 yards and won the NFL **rookie** of the year award.

Following the season, the city of Houston got a special NFL treat, when Reliant Stadium was the site of Super Bowl XXXVIII. The game brought NFL royalty to the city and gave more energy to the Texans' fans.

In 2004, the Texans put a hurt on division rival Tennessee, knocking off the Titans twice. It was the first time the young team had swept another AFC South team. Houston's seven total wins and third-place division finish that year were all-time bests. Andre Johnson set a team record with 1,142 receiving yards. Davis was among the NFL leaders with 13 rushing touchdowns.

However, building an NFL expansion team into a playoff regular takes time and a lot of

Despite gaining only 47 yards, the Texans beat Pittsburgh 24–6 in a 2002 game. How did they do it? Aaron Glenn returned two interceptions for touchdowns, and fellow cornerback Kenny Wright brought back a fumble recovery for a score.

Domanick Williams (who originally was known as Domanick Davis) is the club's top career rusher.

energy. Casserly and Capers built a solid foundation, but in 2006, the Texans turned to longtime Denver Broncos offensive coordinator Gary Kubiak to serve as the second head coach in team history. The

NFL quarterbacks have to be ready for defensive end Mario Williams' crunching hits.

club also hired former Broncos assistant general manager Rick Smith to become the youngest general manager in the NFL.

The Texans raised eyebrows around the country when they passed over **Heisman Trophy**-winning running back Reggie Bush from USC with the first selection in the 2006 NFL draft and instead tabbed North Carolina State defensive end Mario Williams to anchor their defense. With their next pick in that draft, the Texans selected Alabama's All-America linebacker, DeMeco Ryans.

Kubiak and his young Texans team struggled in 2006, but saw great improvement throughout the season. The team finished with back-to-back victories over the eventual Super Bowl-champion Indianapolis Colts (27–24) and the Cleveland Browns (14–6). Ryans was named the Associated Press defensive rookie of the year.

In 2007, Houston replaced Carr with Matt Schaub, who came over in a trade with the Atlanta Falcons. Louisville defensive tackle Amobi Okoye, who was only 19 years old, became the youngest player ever taken in the first round of the NFL draft when the Texans chose him with the 10th overall selection.

Although Houston fans were extremely disappointed a year earlier with the selection of Williams, the massive defensive end emerged as a truly game-changing player in 2007. He tied for third in the league with a club-record 14 **sacks,** including a Texans' single-game record 3.5 sacks in a 31–13 victory over the Broncos.

The Texans hope that young quarterback Matt Schaub can take them to the playoffs for the first time in their history.

Williams and Ryans, who was selected to start in the Pro Bowl, led the Texans to an 8–8 record, the best in team history. With such a young and talented **roster,** the rest of the AFC has been put on notice that Houston is an emerging force. The Texans are on the verge of stamping their brand among the NFL's **elite** teams.

CHAPTER TWO
THE INDIANAPOLIS COLTS

Since 2002, the Colts have put together one of the greatest runs of success in NFL history, highlighted by their dominating 29–17 victory over the Chicago Bears in Super Bowl XLI in the 2006 season. Indianapolis had waited 36 years to return to the top of the NFL after defeating the Dallas Cowboys in Super Bowl V.

Colts quarterback Peyton Manning passed for 247 yards, including a 53-yard touchdown to receiver Reggie Wayne, to earn MVP honors in Super Bowl XLI. Manning wasn't Indianapolis' only star in 2006. The Colts' Tony Dungy became the first African-American coach to lead his team to a Super Bowl victory.

Running back Joseph Addai was the NFL's rookie rushing leader with 1,081 yards during the regular season and set a Super Bowl record for running backs with 10 receptions. Marvin

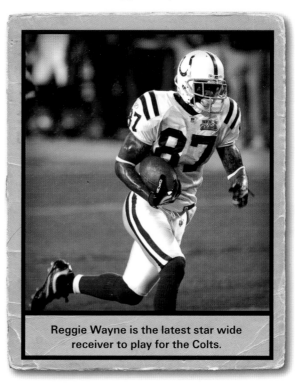

Reggie Wayne is the latest star wide receiver to play for the Colts.

Harrison, Manning's favorite target and one of the greatest receivers in league history, earned his eighth **consecutive** Pro Bowl selection. And end Dwight Freeney, the club's all-time sack leader, dominated on defense.

Winning the Super Bowl MVP award put a cherry on the top of a probable Pro Football Hall of Fame career for Manning, who started every game his first 10 seasons in the league (1998–2007) and earned eight Pro Bowl selections. In fact, Manning threw more passes (5,405) for more yards (41,626) and more touchdowns (306) than any other quarterback in NFL history did in his first 10 years.

If Manning does indeed make the Pro Football Hall of Fame, he would join 12 other Colts, including stars from the Baltimore **era** such as Raymond Berry, Art Donovan, Ted Hendricks, John Mackey, Gino Marchetti, Lenny Moore, Jim Parker, John Unitas, and head coaches Weeb Ewbank and Don Shula.

Indianapolis followed its Super Bowl season with another brilliant season in 2007. The team won 13 games in the regular season, and safety Bob Sanders was named the NFL defensive player of the year. From 2003 to 2007, Indianapolis set a league record with five consecutive 12-win seasons, won five consecutive AFC South titles, and played in two AFC Championship Games.

That's a long way from the club's humble beginnings in 1953. That year, the NFL awarded a group of Baltimore businessman a **defunct**

Weeb Ewbank, who guided the Colts from 1954 to 1962, is the only coach to win championships in both the NFL and the AFL. Ewbank led the Colts to titles in 1958 and 1959. In 1968, he coached the New York Jets to the AFL title and a victory in Super Bowl III—over his old team, the Colts!

Johnny Unitas was a legendary quarterback. He led the Colts to back-to-back NFL championships in 1958 and 1959.

franchise called the Dallas Texans. The Texans won only one game in their final season in 1952, and Colts weren't much better, winning only three times in '53. But Ewbank took over as coach in 1954 and began assembling a team with some great players. They included quarterback Unitas, receiver Berry, tackle Parker, and defensive end Marchetti. The team improved quickly and made it all the way to the top of the NFL in 1958.

The Colts won Super Bowl V when Jim O'Brien (80) made this field goal in the final seconds.

The NFL Championship Game of 1958 is still known as "The Greatest Game Ever Played." The Colts faced the New York Giants in Yankee Stadium in one of the first title games ever broadcast on TV. A huge audience saw a thrilling game. The Colts tied it at 17–17 with a field goal in the final seconds. But this was a championship, and there had to be a winner. For the first time, **sudden-death overtime** would be used to decide the winner. The first team to score would win.

Unitas was superb. As a quarterback, he has had few equals in league history. He was an expert at moving his team quickly with little time left. In overtime, he marched the Colts down the field. Though they were close enough for an easy field goal, he chose to go for the touchdown. After completing a pass to the 1-yard line, Unitas handed off to Alan "The Horse" Ameche. The Horse rode into the end zone, the Colts were champions, and the NFL entered a new, TV-filled era.

The Colts repeated as champs in 1959. They tried for the championship again in 1964, but lost the title game. In 1968, packed with new stars that included running back Tom Matte and tight end Mackey, the Colts put on a rare show. The team finished the regular season with only one loss. The defense tied a record by allowing only 144 points. After winning the NFL title easily, Baltimore faced the AFL champs, the New York Jets, in Super Bowl III. Though Baltimore was heavily **favored,** the Jets pulled off one of the greatest upsets in sports history. They defeated a team many consider one of the best ever, 16–7. It was the game that made Jets quarterback Joe Namath a star.

Two years later, the Colts returned to Super Bowl V. This time, Baltimore emerged as champions when rookie kicker Jim O'Brien nailed a game-winning field goal with five seconds left.

The Colts returned to the playoffs three more times in the 1970s. Their stars included running back Lydell Mitchell, who became the team's first 1,000-yard runner in 1975. Quarterback Bert Jones was among the NFL's best. However, Baltimore didn't reach the big game, and the team faded later in the decade.

In 1984, the team underwent its biggest change. Though teams are supposed to alert the league when they move, Colts owner Irsay didn't bother with that detail. He worked out a deal to move his team to Indianapolis. Then he headed west before anyone knew what was going on. Baltimore fans, who loved their team no matter how well it did, were devastated. Pro football didn't come back to "Charm City" until 1995, when the Cleveland Browns became the Baltimore Ravens.

In Indianapolis, the Colts moved to an indoor stadium now called the RCA Dome. The team's brightest moment was in 1995 when it came one play short of reaching another Super Bowl. Led by quarterback Jim Harbaugh, the Colts had earned a **wild-card** playoff spot and reached the AFC Championship Game against Pittsburgh. The Colts fell to the Steelers 20–16. Harbaugh's long pass on the final play was nearly caught by a Colts' receiver in the end zone.

In 1998, the Colts found the big reason for their modern-day success by picking Manning with the first overall choice in the draft. Manning, the son of former NFL star quarterback Archie Manning, quickly surpassed his father's achievements and staked his claim as one of the game's best passers. He set numerous rookie passing records in 1998 and led the Colts to a division title in 1999. From 1998 to 2005, Manning, receiver Marvin Harrison, and running back Edgerrin James formed one of the NFL's top offensive trios.

In 2004, Manning teamed with Harrison and the Colts' other talented receivers to break a record many thought could never be topped. Flinging

The Colts played in the RCA Dome from 1984 (their first season in Indianapolis) through 2007. They moved into the new Lucas Oil Stadium for the 2008 season.

Quarterback Peyton Manning and his right arm have kept the Colts among the NFL's top teams during the 2000s.

touchdown after touchdown, Manning set a new all-time, single-season record with 49 touchdown passes. (Manning's mark eventually was broken by Tom Brady, who passed for 50 touchdowns for the New England Patriots in 2007.)

Of course, for a team that likes to move, all that flying up and down the field was nothing new!

CHAPTER THREE

THE JACKSONVILLE JAGUARS

Jacksonville is the second-smallest city to play host to an NFL team (behind only Green Bay and its Packers). But even though the Jacksonville Jaguars have only been in the league since 1995, they already have made a big mark on the NFL.

In Jacksonville's brief NFL history, they have played in two AFC Championship Games, been to the playoffs six times, and even hosted Super Bowl XXXIX in 2005.

When the NFL announced that it was expanding, many cities tried to earn one of the teams. In 1993, Jacksonville was awarded one of the expansion teams, with local businessman Wayne Weaver as the owner. Weaver had two years to get his team ready for its first game, and the first thing he did was hire a coach. Tom Coughlin

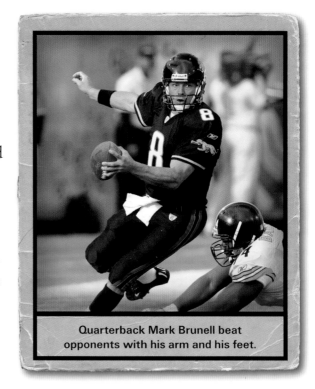

Quarterback Mark Brunell beat opponents with his arm and his feet.

had been a success at Boston College. Now he was given free rein to create an NFL team from scratch. The league gave Jacksonville extra draft picks and allowed the team to choose some players from existing teams. Still, few people expected the Jaguars to be very good any time soon. It can take years to build a quality NFL team. Coughlin and Weaver were in a hurry, however.

Their quarterback was left-handed Mark Brunell, who combined laser-like passing with great **scrambling** ability. His receivers, Jimmy Smith and Keenan McCardell, would become Pro Bowl players. Brunell helped the Jaguars win their first-ever game in the fifth week of the first season. They won three more games that year and finished their initial season at 4–12. In the draft, they had solidified their defense with linebacker Kevin Hardy. They also chose superb offensive tackle Tony Boselli to help protect Brunell.

The 1996 season, only Jacksonville's second, would prove to be a Cinderella story . . . and the beginning of good times down South. The Jaguars were 8–7 going into the final game of the season.

If they beat Atlanta in that game, they would earn a wild-card playoff spot. However, the Falcons, trailing by one point, drove near the Jaguars' goal line for a short field-goal try. Atlanta's kicker, Morten Andersen, was one of the NFL's all-time best. He had not missed a kick inside 30 yards all season. Guess what? He missed this one, and the Jaguars were suddenly, surprisingly, in the playoffs at the tender NFL age of two.

The surprises just kept coming. The Jaguars traveled to Buffalo, where the hometown Bills had never lost a playoff game. Jacksonville battled all game long, and the score was tied at 27–27 late in the game. Then Jacksonville recovered a Buffalo fumble. Kicker Mike Hollis nailed a 45-yard field goal, and the baby Jaguars won the game!

They could only celebrate briefly, however, for up next came the powerful Denver Broncos. Denver had posted an AFC-best 13–3 record. Its star quarterback, John Elway, was on his way to a Hall of Fame career. However, the Jaguars' defense kept Elway bottled up for most of the game. In the fourth quarter, Brunell led a key touchdown drive, twice scrambling for first downs. Jacksonville needed the 10-point lead it created, because Elway and Denver scored again. But the Broncos needed more than that and couldn't get it. Once again, the Cinderella team was a winner by a 30–27 score.

Though the Jaguars lost in the AFC Championship Game to New England, it was a monumental start for a young team. No other expansion team had ever played for a conference title so quickly. (Second-year Carolina also played for the NFC title the same year.)

Things just kept getting better. Jacksonville's high-scoring offense kept rolling, and the team posted 11 wins in each of the next two seasons. In 1998, the Jaguars were helped by rookie running back Fred Taylor, who gave Brunell a new weapon on offense. Taylor rushed for 1,223 yards and scored 17 touchdowns.

In 1995, Steve Beuerlein was the starting quarterback for the first regular-season game in Jaguars' history. But he soon gave way to Mark Brunell, a youngster Jacksonville got from Green Bay in the club's first trade.

Running back Fred Taylor has been going strong since he joined the Jaguars as a first-round draft pick in 1998.

Taylor and Brunell led the Jaguars to the best record in the entire NFL in 1999 at 14–2. Their offense scored the second-most points in the conference, while their defense gave up the fewest. In a divisional playoff game against Miami, Jacksonville exploded for 62 points. It was the second-highest total in a playoff game in NFL history. The only topper was the 73 points scored in a 1940 game by the Chicago Bears against the Washington Redskins. The 55-point victory margin

(Miami scored 7 points) was the second-most ever, too. It was the most points any Miami team had ever given up in a game. The game's highlight play was Taylor's 90-yard touchdown run, the longest scoring run in NFL playoff history.

Unfortunately, Jacksonville should have saved some of those points for the AFC Championship Game. There, the Jaguars lost to the Tennessee Titans 33–14. Cinderella suddenly saw her ride to the Super Bowl turn into a pumpkin.

The loss of some keys players led to down years for Jacksonville. From 2000 to 2002, the Jaguars won only six games each season. In 2003, former NFL linebacker Jack Del Rio took over from Tom Coughlin as the team's head coach.

Del Rio helped restore the roar in Jacksonville, guiding the team to 12–4 record and a playoff spot in his third season (2005) and an 11–5 record and a **postseason** appearance in 2007. The Jaguars' trademarks under Del Rio have been a two-headed offensive attack led by Taylor and another exciting runner, Maurice Jones-Drew. In his first 10 seasons, Taylor racked up more than 10,000 rushing yards. In 2007, he was rewarded with his first Pro Bowl appearance after rushing for 1,202 yards and a career-best 5.4 yards per carry.

The 5-foot-7 Jones-Drew is a threat to score every time he touches the ball. As a rookie he totaled an amazing 2,250 yards rushing, receiving, and returning kicks, and he scored 16 touchdowns. In 2007, Jones-Drew again totaled more than 2,000 yards and scored nine touchdowns.

Jacksonville lost to only one team during the entire 1999 season: division rival Tennessee. The Jaguars won 15 of the 18 games (including postseason) that they played that year. But they could not overcome the Titans in any of their three meetings, including the AFC title game.

Former NFL linebacker Jack Del Rio, who took over as the Jaguars' coach in 2003, knows how to fire up his players!

Speedy and strong, running back Maurice Jones-Drew is hard to catch—and even harder to bring down.

Add an extremely tough defense, especially a powerful defensive line, to Taylor's and Jones-Drew's explosiveness, and the only way is up for the Jaguars. Jacksonville is like the little train engine. The Jaguars just keep saying, "I think we can, I think we can…" reach the top of the NFL. The rest of the league better take notice.

CHAPTER FOUR
THE TENNESSEE TITANS

F ans of the Tennessee Titans have enjoyed a variety of historic moments since the team moved to Nashville from Houston (where it had been named the Oilers since 1960) a decade ago. Titans fans have seen a new state-of-the-art stadium built and witnessed a "Music City Miracle" in 1999. Later in that same postseason, Titans fans saw their team come just inches short of scoring a game-tying touchdown on the final play of Super Bowl XXXIV.

Most recently, Titans fans have seen the youngest quarterback in franchise history, former Heisman Trophy winner Vince Young, lead the team to the playoffs. Young also was chosen to the Pro Bowl and named NFL rookie of the year following the 2006 season.

Since the franchise was formed as a founding member of the American Football League in 1960, only one man has owned the team. Bud Adams was one of several businessmen who started a new pro football league in 1960

Owner Bud Adams moved his Houston Oilers' franchise to Tennessee in 1997.

Earl Campbell was a powerful running back for Houston from 1978 to 1984. He is a member of the Pro Football Hall of Fame.

to rival the established NFL. The AFL started with eight teams, including Adams' Houston Oilers. Led by quarterback George Blanda, Houston won AFL titles in 1960 and 1961. Blanda would later become famous as the NFL's "old man," playing until he was 48 years old.

The next big news in Oilers' history came in 1968, when they moved into the Houston Astrodome. The enormous indoor stadium was called "The Eighth Wonder of the World." The Oilers were the first pro football team to play indoors. In 1970, the Oilers became part of the NFL along with the nine other AFL teams. Houston joined the AFC's Central Division.

The team didn't show much promise until 1978. A new coach, Bum Phillips, led the way while wearing his famous cowboy boots. Quarterback Dan Pastorini was tough and strong-armed. And the Oilers welcomed a rookie who would become one of the NFL's all-time great players: running back Earl Campbell. He burst onto the scene and led the AFC with 1,450 rushing yards. The team finished 10–6, and the yell "Luv Ya Blue" (a team color) roared through the Astrodome. Houston made it to the AFC Championship Game before losing to Pittsburgh.

The next season, 1979, was more of the same. Campbell rambled for a rushing title, and the Oilers played for a spot in the Super Bowl. But again, they fell to the Steelers. In 1980, Campbell pounded for 1,934 yards. But once more, the Oilers fell in the playoffs.

The 1980s were a lost cause for Houston until the team signed quarterback Warren Moon, who eventually would be elected to the Pro Football Hall of Fame. With Moon's slingshot arm and a powerful defense, the Oilers were the only NFL team to make the playoffs every year from 1987 to 1993. However, in each of those seasons, they fell short of their ultimate goal, the Super Bowl. The worst playoff loss came in 1992. Ahead of Buffalo 35–3 in the second half, they allowed the Bills to tie the game. Buffalo went on to win in overtime to complete the greatest comeback in NFL history.

The Oilers bounced back to go 12–4 in 1993, but another playoff loss was a bitter one. Moon left the team in the off-season, along with several defensive stars. In 1994, the Oilers were 2–14, marking the worst single-season turnaround in league history.

In 1996, Adams tried something new to shake the team up. The Astrodome was an aging stadium, and people were not coming out as they had in years past. He announced he was moving the team to Tennessee in 1997. It was an odd period for the team. In 1996, they were the Houston Oilers. In 1997, they were the Tennessee Oilers and played in the Liberty Bowl in Memphis. In 1998, still the Oilers, they played in Nashville's Vanderbilt University Stadium. In 1999, they became the Tennessee Titans and played in the brand-new Coliseum (now called LP Field), also in Nashville.

The new digs suited the Titans just fine, and years of playoff frustration came to an end in 1999.

Jeff Fisher is the only coach the Tennessee Titans have had. He took over in the second half of the 1994 season, when the club was still the Houston Oilers.

Strrrettttch! **Kevin Dyson came very close to scoring the tying touchdown on the final play of Super Bowl XXXIV.**

Coach Jeff Fisher had built a championship team. Quarterback Steve McNair and running back Eddie George keyed the offense. The team's 13–3 record was a franchise-best and good for a wild-card spot against the Bills. In that game, the Titans pulled off the Music City Miracle. Trailing by three points with just 16 seconds to go, they took a kickoff and, using a cross-field lateral, returned it for a game-winning touchdown. They went on to defeat the Colts and Jaguars to earn a spot in Super Bowl XXXIV against the St. Louis Rams.

For the first time since winning the AFL crown 38 years earlier, Bud Adams' team would play for a title. Most experts gave Tennessee little chance, though. The Rams had lit up scoreboards around the

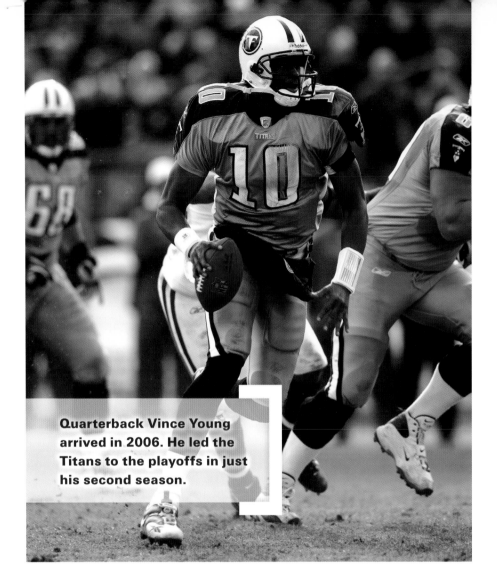

Quarterback Vince Young arrived in 2006. He led the Titans to the playoffs in just his second season.

NFL that season, leading the league with 526 points. However, the Titans gave the Rams all they could handle. With a little more than two minutes left, Tennessee capped a rally from a 16–0 **deficit** to tie the score at 16–16 on Al Del Greco's field goal.

The Rams stunned the Titans with a 73-yard bomb from Kurt Warner to Isaac Bruce to take the lead. McNair had less than two minutes to try to match Warner, and he nearly did it. The key play of the final drive came when McNair barely avoided being sacked and rifled a 16-yard pass to the Rams' 10-yard line. There were just six seconds left and time for one more play.

Vince Young is the only quarterback since 1966 to rush for more than 500 yards in his rookie season. He gained 552 yards and ran in 7 touchdowns in 2006.

With almost four decades of frustration hanging on the line, McNair zipped a pass to receiver Kevin Dyson at the five. It seemed as if Dyson would go in to score. But Rams linebacker Mike Jones made one of the best plays in Super Bowl history. He wrapped up the speedy receiver and tackled him inside the one-yard line. The game ended with the Titans inches away from a tying score.

Though they fell short that year and won only seven games in 2001, the Titans' Super Bowl season launched the Titans on an upward path. In 2002, the team won the AFC South again. In 2003, Tennessee won 12 games and earned a wild-card playoff spot. During this run, McNair remained the key player for the team. He showed his toughness by overcoming several injuries to continue to lead the team. However, even he could not carry the Titans back to the Super Bowl.

In 2004, injuries finally knocked McNair out for several games, along with other key players. The team won only five games. A bright light was the play of receiver Drew Bennett. He caught 11 touchdown passes, and his 233 receiving yards in a game against the Chiefs set a club record.

Two years later, Young arrived. Late in his rookie season, he led the Titans on a six-game winning streak. Then, in 2007, he helped the team win 10 games and earn a wild-card playoff spot.

Although the season ended with a loss to San Diego in the opening round of the postseason, the presence of the dynamic Young has NFL fans in Tennessee hopeful for the future.

TIME LINE

1953
Baltimore Colts join the NFL

1958
Colts win NFL championship

1959
Colts repeat as NFL champions

1940　1950　1960　1970

1960
Houston Oilers founded as part of the AFL (they moved to Tennessee in 1997); win AFL championship

1961
Oilers repeat as AFL champs

1968
Colts win NFL title, but lose to AFL-champion New York Jets in Super Bowl III

1970
Colts win Super Bowl V over the Dallas Cowboys

1996

Jaguars advance to AFC Championship Game in only their second season; they lose to New England

1997

Houston Oilers move to Tennessee and in 1999 become the Titans

1995

Jacksonville Jaguars begin play in AFC

1999

Jaguars return to AFC title game, but lose again, this time to the Titans

1995

Colts reach AFC Championship Game, lose to Steelers

1980   1990   2000   2010

2002

Houston Texans begin play as expansion team

1984

Colts move from Baltimore to Indianapolis

2004

Colts' Peyton Manning sets NFL record (since broken) with 49 touchdown passes

2006

Colts win the Super Bowl for the first time since moving to Indianapolis, beating Chicago in game XLI

STAT STUFF

TEAM RECORDS (THROUGH 2007)*

Team	All-time Record	Number of Titles (Most Recent)	Number of Times in Playoffs	Top Coach (Wins)
Houston	32–64–0	0	0	Dom Capers (18)
Indianapolis	432–401–7	4 (2006)	21	Tony Dungy (80)
Jacksonville	118–101–0	0	6	Tom Coughlin (72)
Tennessee	364–386–6	2 (1961)	20	Jeff Fisher (120)

*includes AFL and NFL totals

AFC SOUTH CAREER LEADERS (THROUGH 2007)

Category	Name (Years With Team)	Total
Houston		
Rushing yards	Domanick Williams (2003–06)	3,195
Passing yards	David Carr (2002–06)	13,391
Touchdown passes	David Carr (2002–06)	59
Receptions	Andre Johnson (2003–07)	371
Touchdowns	Domanick Williams (2003–06)	28
Scoring	Kris Brown (2002–07)	537
Indianapolis		
Rushing yards	Edgerrin James (1999–2005)	9,226
Passing yards	Peyton Manning (1998–2007)	41,626
Touchdown passes	Peyton Manning (1998–2007)	306
Receptions	Marvin Harrison (1996–2007)	1,042
Touchdowns	Marvin Harrison (1996–2007)	123
Scoring	Mike Vanderjagt (1998–2005)	995
Jacksonville		
Rushing yards	Fred Taylor (1998–2007)	10,715
Passing yards	Mark Brunell (1995–2003)	25,698
Touchdown passes	Mark Brunell (1995–2003)	144
Receptions	Jimmy Smith (1995–2005)	862
Touchdowns	Jimmy Smith (1995–2005)	69
	Fred Taylor (1998–2007)	69
Scoring	Mike Hollis (1995–2001)	764
Tennessee		
Rushing yards	Eddie George (1996–2003)	10,009
Passing yards	Warren Moon (1984–1993)	33,685
Touchdown passes	Warren Moon (1984–1993)	196
Receptions	Ernest Givins (1986–1994)	542
Touchdowns	Eddie George (1996–2003)	74
Scoring	Al Del Greco (1991–2000)	1,060

MEMBERS OF THE PRO FOOTBALL HALL OF FAME

Player	Position	Date Inducted
Houston		
None		
Indianapolis		
Raymond Berry	End	1973
Eric Dickerson	Running Back	1999
Art Donovan	Defensive Tackle	1968
Weeb Ewbank	Coach	1978
Ted Hendricks	Linebacker	1990
John Mackey	Tight End	1992
Gino Marchetti	Defensive End	1972
Lenny Moore	Flanker/Running Back	1975
Jim Parker	Guard/Tackle	1973
Joe Perry	Fullback	1969
Don Shula	Coach	1997
Johnny Unitas	Quarterback	1979
Jacksonville		
None		
Tennessee		
Elvin Bethea	Defensive End	2003
George Blanda	Quarterback/Kicker	1981
Earl Campbell	Running Back	1991
Dave Casper	Tight End	2002
Sid Gillman	Coach	1993
Ken Houston	Safety	1986
John Henry Johnson	Running Back	1987
Charlie Joiner	Wide Receiver	1996
Bruce Matthews	Offensive Line	2007
Warren Moon	Quarterback	2006
Mike Munchak	Tight End	2001

GLOSSARY

associates—people you work with

consecutive—in a row; one after the other

deficit—the score or amount of points by which a team is losing

defunct—a company or group that is no longer in business

draft—held each April, this is when NFL teams choose college players to join their teams; the teams with the worst records the prior season choose first, but draft picks can be traded to move a team's draft order

elite—among the very best, of very high quality

era—a period of time known for a particular event or person

expansion team—in the NFL, the term used for a new team added to the league

favored—in sports, this describes a team that most people think will win a game

franchise—more than just a team, it is the entire organization that is a member of a professional sports league

free agents—players who have completed their contracts with one team and are free to sign with any other team

fumble—when a ballcarrier drops the football during a play

Heisman Trophy—a yearly award given to the best college football player

interceptions—passes caught by the defense instead of the offense

playoffs—after the regular schedule, these are the games played to determine the champion

postseason—the period in which the playoffs are held

retired—taken out of service, not to be used again

rival—someone who competes for the same goal

rookie—an athlete in his or her first season as a professional

roster—the list of players on a team

sacks—when quarterbacks are tackled behind the line of scrimmage

scrambling—when a quarterback runs out of the pocket and carries the ball downfield or avoids tacklers to make a pass

sudden-death overtime—when an NFL game is tied, an extra period is played during which any score by either team wins the game

Super Bowl—the NFL's championship game, played in late January or early February at a different stadium each year

wild-card—a team that makes the playoffs without winning a division title

FIND OUT MORE

Books

Frisch, Aaron. *The History of the Tennessee Titans.*
Mankato, Minn.: Creative Education, 2005.

Hawkes, Brian. *The History of the Jacksonville Jaguars.*
Mankato, Minn.: Creative Education, 2005.

Ladewski, Paul. *National Football League Superstars 2007.*
New York: Scholastic, 2007.

Marini, Matt. *Football Top 10.* New York: DK
Publishing, 2002.

Nichols, John. *The History of the Houston Texans.*
Mankato, Minn: Creative Education, 2005.

Polzer, Tim. *Peyton Manning: Leader On and Off the Field.*
Berkeley Heights, N.J.: Enslow Publishers, 2006.

Stewart, Mark. *The Indianapolis Colts.* Chicago:
Norwood House Press, 2007.

On the Web

Visit our Web site for lots of links about the AFC South:
http://www.childsworld.com/links

Note to Parents, Teachers, and Librarians: We routinely verify our Web links to make sure they are safe, active sites—so encourage your readers to check them out!

INDEX